CAVES and CAVERNS

Gail Gibbons

Harcourt Brace & Company

SAN DIEGO   NEW YORK   LONDON

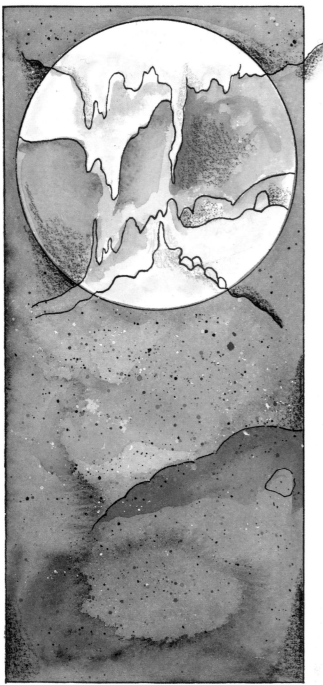

For Eva, Eric, Emily, and Paul Murray

Special thanks to Ron Kerbo,
Cave Specialist for the National Park Service
Santa Fe, New Mexico

Copyright © 1993 by Gail Gibbons

Requests for permission to make copies
of any part of the work should be mailed to:
Permissions Department,
Harcourt Brace & Company, 8th Floor,
Orlando, Florida 32887.

Library of Congress Cataloging-in-Publication Data
Gibbons, Gail.
Caves and caverns/Gail Gibbons — 1st ed.
p.   cm.
Summary: Text and labeled illustrations describe
the formation and physical features of various kinds
of caves, with a brief section on spelunking.
ISBN 0-15-226820-0
1. Caves — Juvenile literature.   [1. Caves.]   I. Title.
GB601.2.G52   1993
551.4'47 — dc20   92-760

First edition
A B C D E

Printed in Singapore

Deep down in the earth, people have found dark hollow places. They are called caves. Caves appear in the sides of hills or mountains, or sometimes they begin from the surface of the land and extend downward.

Some caves are small, and others
are big.

Some are huge! Thousands and thousands of caves and caverns exist in many parts of the world.

Caves and caverns can be millions of years old, but they are constantly being changed and created. Sea caves are made by the pounding of ocean waves. The waves dig out the seashore cliffs, grinding away at them year after year with sand, pebbles, rocks, and boulders. This constant pounding wears the softer rock away.

SEA CAVE

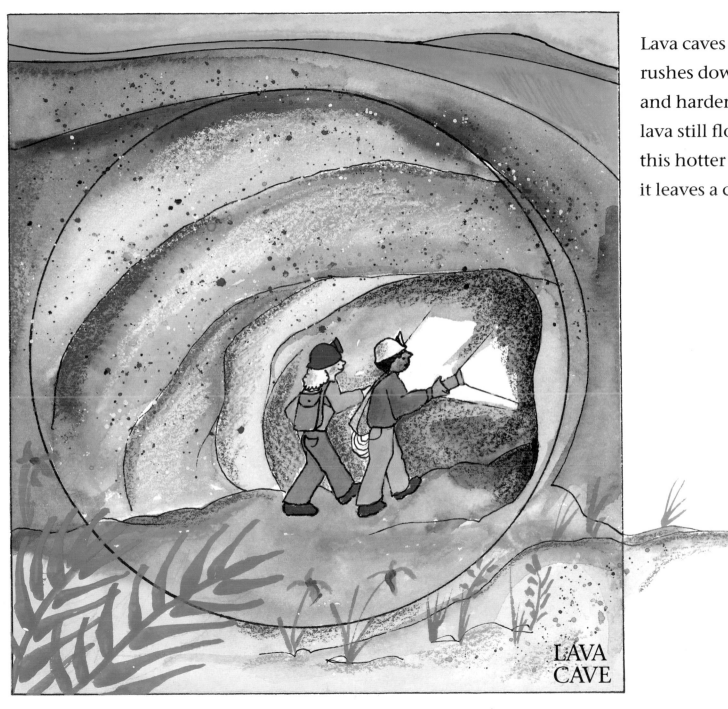

LAVA
CAVE

Lava caves are made when lava rushes down the sides of volcanoes and hardens on the surface. Hot lava still flows underneath. When this hotter lava finally flows away, it leaves a cave behind.

There are ice caves, too. They are formed by streams that erode tunnels under mountain glaciers. The water in these streams comes from melted ice on the surface that seeps through cracks. Some ice caves begin as rock caves and then are coated with ice.

ICE CAVE

LIMESTONE
OR
SOLUTION
CAVE

A limestone cave, also called a solution cave, is the most common type of cave. Limestone caves begin to form when rain falls to the earth, collecting carbon dioxide from the air.

CARBON DIOXIDE

As rainwater trickles through the soil, it picks up more carbon dioxide. The water and the carbon dioxide mix together to become an acid solution called carbonic acid. As this solution seeps through the limestone, it eats away at the soft stone, making small holes.

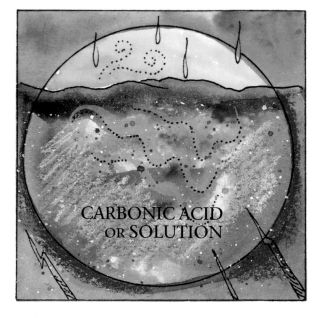

CARBONIC ACID
OR SOLUTION

Many years go by and the holes become bigger . . .

and bigger . . .

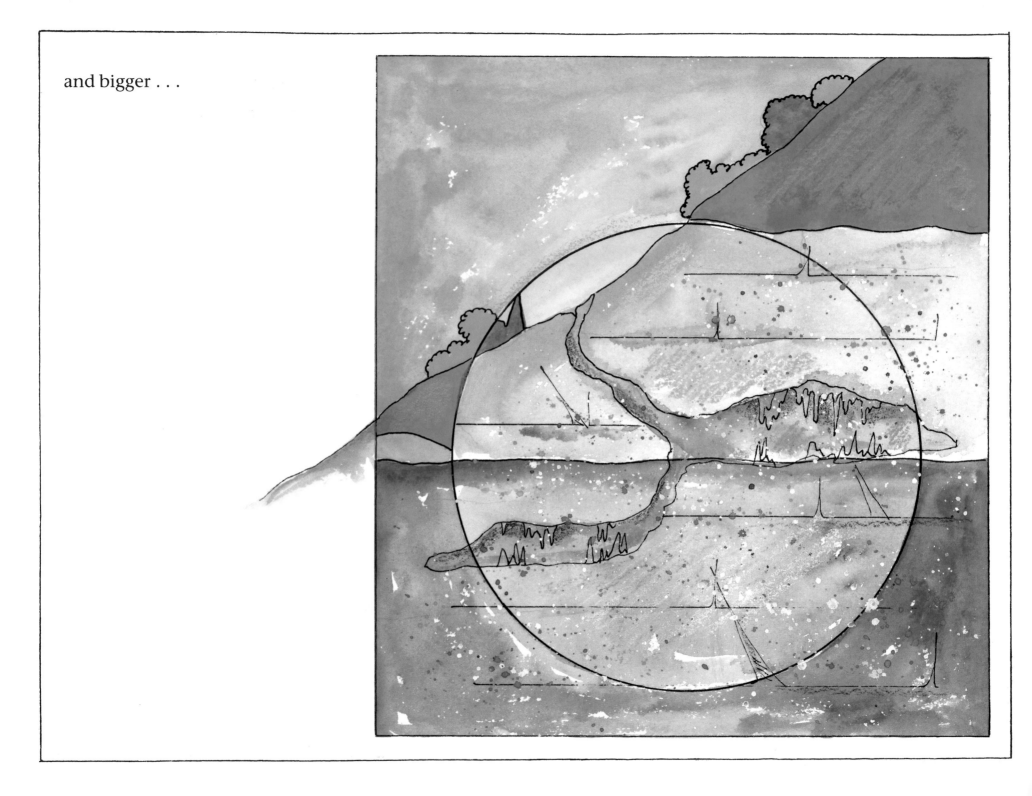

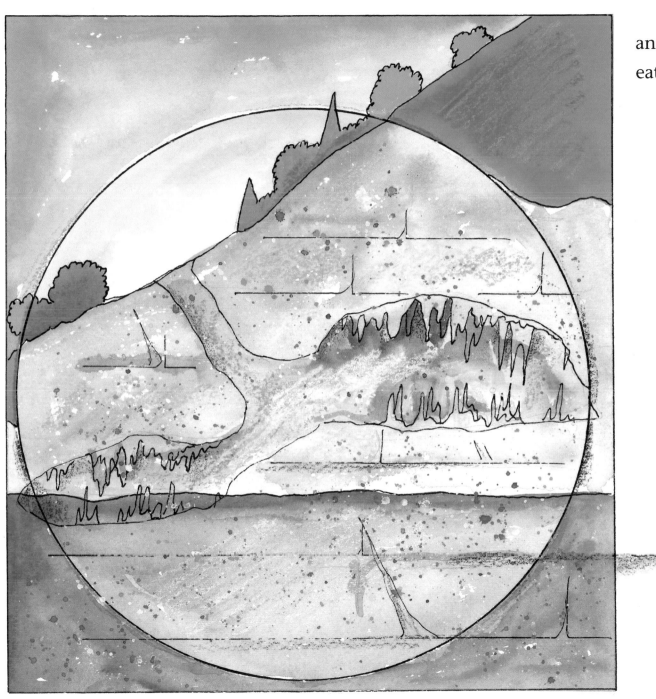

and bigger. The solution keeps eating away at the limestone.

Finally, when the water drains away, air enters the hollow space and begins to form a limestone cave.

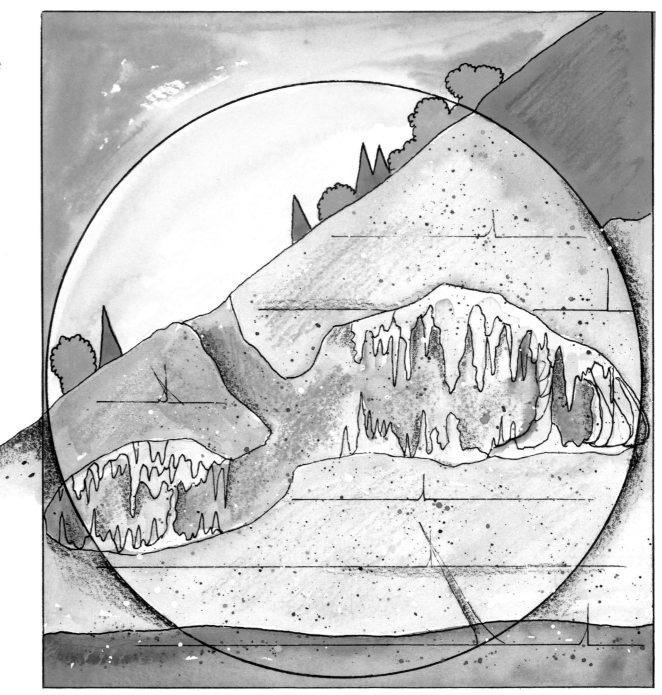

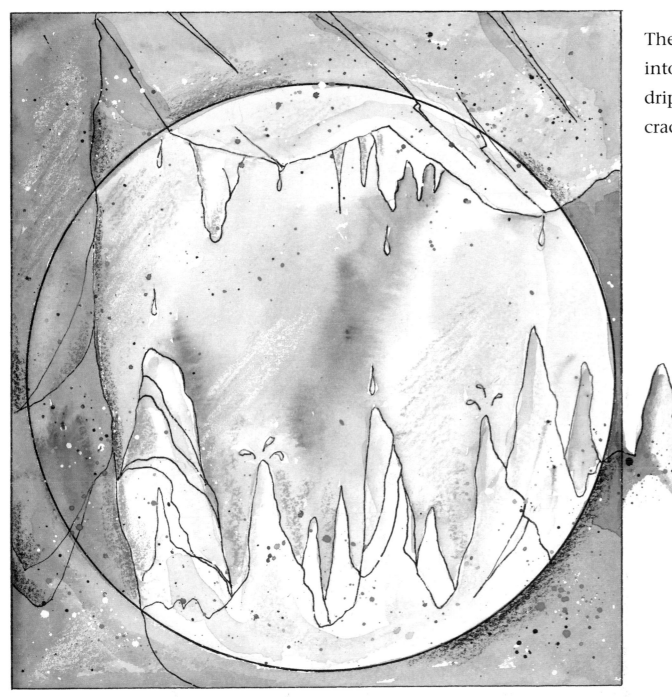

The solution continues to drip into the limestone cave. Drip . . . drip . . . drip . . . It seeps through cracks in the rock.

When a drop dries on the ceiling of a cave, it leaves a tiny bit of calcite crystal. Another drop follows. It leaves behind calcite crystal, too. Drop after drop, the calcite crystals collect in the same spot. These crystals build up to form a stone icicle called a stalactite.

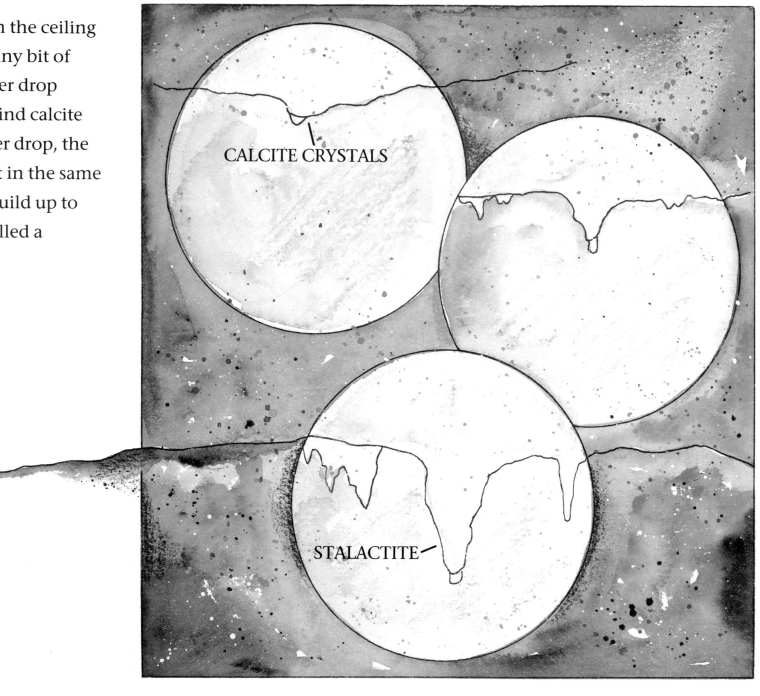

CALCITE CRYSTALS

STALACTITE

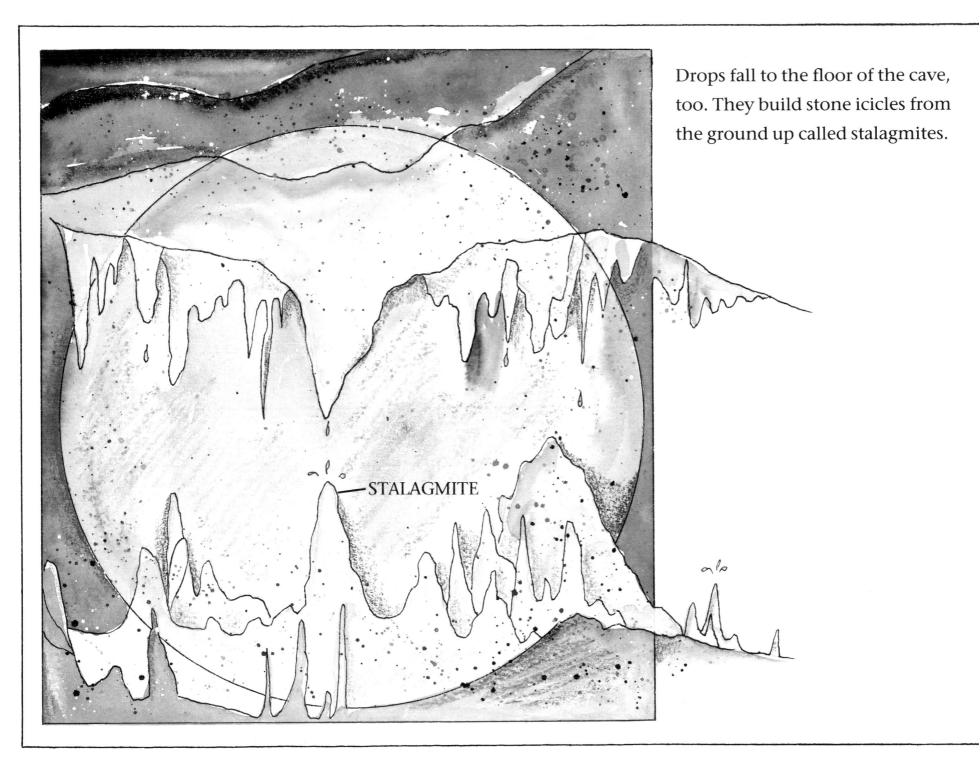

Drops fall to the floor of the cave, too. They build stone icicles from the ground up called stalagmites.

STALAGMITE

The constant dripping of the solution creates these formations, changing a cave into an amazing place of beauty. When the minerals in the solution change, layers of different colors form, too.

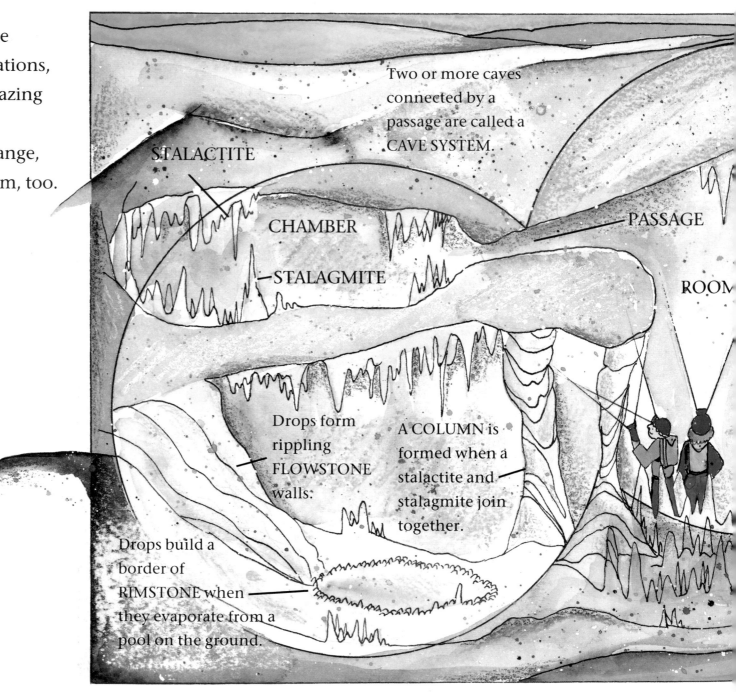

Two or more caves connected by a passage are called a CAVE SYSTEM.

STALACTITE

CHAMBER

STALAGMITE

PASSAGE

ROOM

Drops form rippling FLOWSTONE walls:

A COLUMN is formed when a stalactite and stalagmite join together.

Drops build a border of RIMSTONE when they evaporate from a pool on the ground.

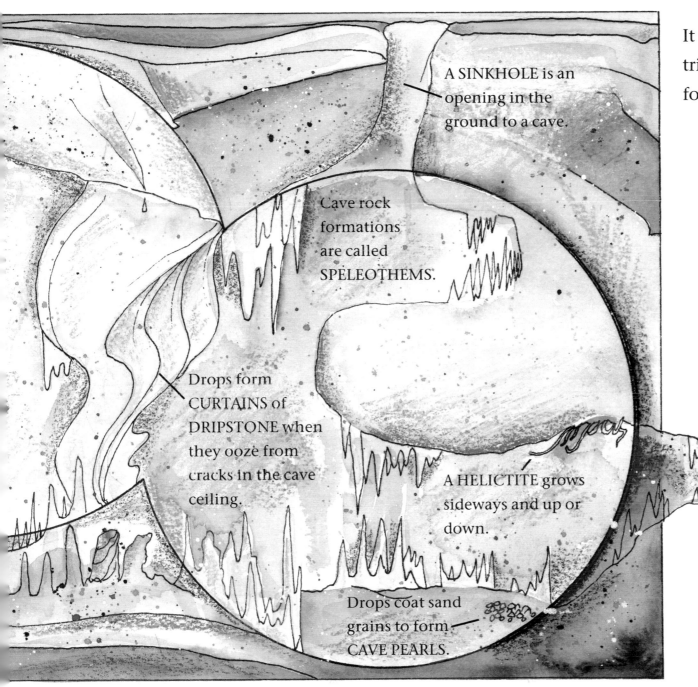

A SINKHOLE is an opening in the ground to a cave.

Cave rock formations are called SPELEOTHEMS.

Drops form CURTAINS of DRIPSTONE when they ooze from cracks in the cave ceiling.

A HELICTITE grows sideways and up or down.

Drops coat sand grains to form CAVE PEARLS.

It takes millions of years and trillions upon trillions of drops to form a limestone cave or cavern.

Spelunca is the Latin word for cave. Speleologists are experts who know a lot about different caves. People who explore caves are called spelunkers or cavers. When cavers first enter a cave, they go into what is called the twilight zone. This area extends from the mouth of the cave to as far as daylight can be seen.

In the twilight zone, it's always a bit cooler than the outside temperature in the summer and milder than the outside temperature in the winter. Often, animals such as birds, snakes, skunks, or mice live in the mouth and twilight zone of a cave. Some green plants grow there, too.

Next, the cavers carefully enter the variable temperature zone. The temperature doesn't change as much here as it does in the twilight zone. Mushrooms, molds, and other fungi grow here. It is dark!

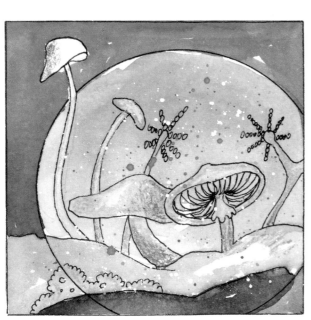

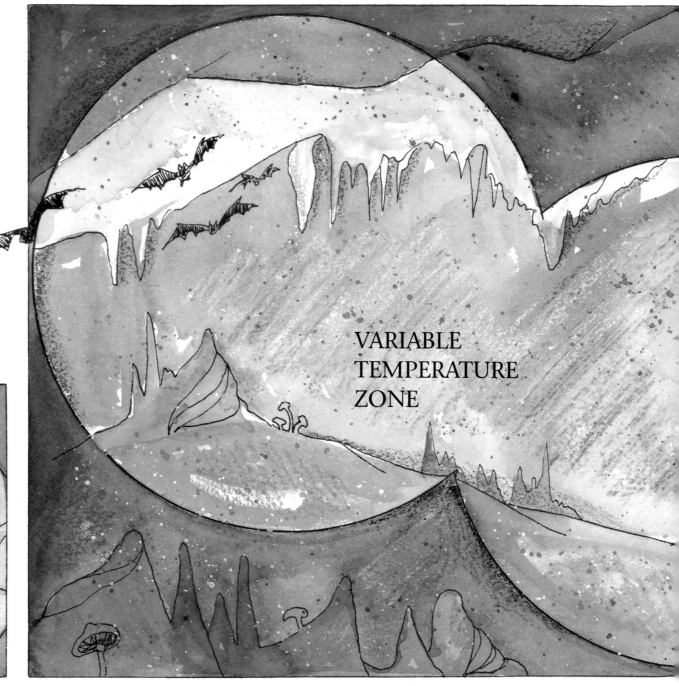

VARIABLE
TEMPERATURE
ZONE

In some caves, bats hang from the ceiling and sleep during the day. At night they fly out of the mouth of the cave to hunt insects. Crickets and salamanders can live inside, too. Green plants cannot live there because they need light to grow.

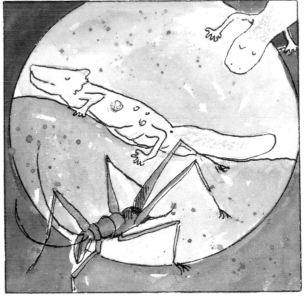

The deepest part of a cave is completely black, pitch-black! This is the constant temperature zone. Air and water stay the same temperature year-round. The air is still. It smells moldy. Everything is moist.

CONSTANT
TEMPERATURE
ZONE

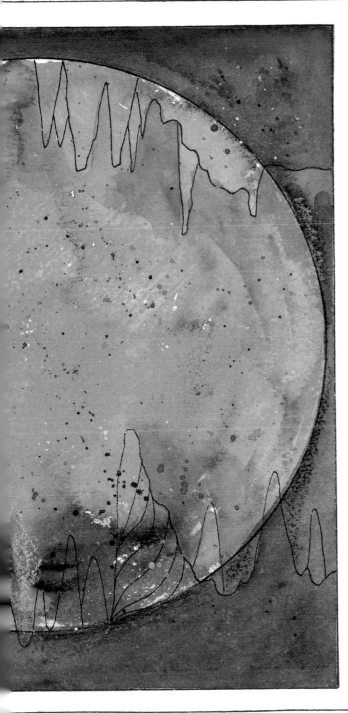

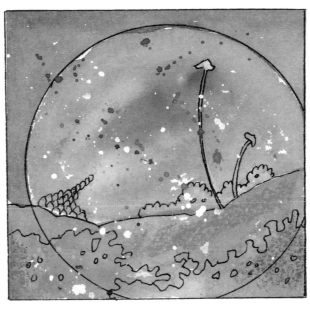

Some bacteria and molds grow here. Strange cave dwellers also live in the constant temperature zone. They are blind. They never need to use their eyes because it is too dark where they live. They are colorless, too. Their bodies don't need protection from sunlight because there isn't any. They rely on touch, sound, and taste to find their food.

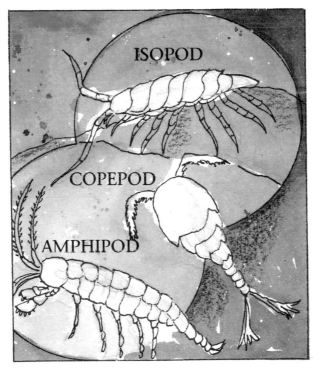

ISOPOD

COPEPOD

AMPHIPOD

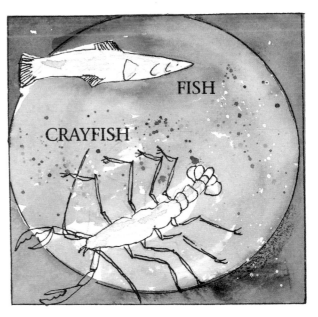

FISH

CRAYFISH

Near cave openings, cavers have found bits of charcoal from long-dead fires, stone knives, broken pieces of pottery, and animal bones. Many thousands of years ago, people lived near the entrances of these caves.

These ancient cave dwellers lived there for protection from weather and dangerous animals. The artifacts tell us how these people lived.

Cavers have also found ancient paintings and drawings. Some are in the darkest parts of caves, where people believed that the gods and spirits they worshiped lived. Cave dwellers made their drawings and paintings for them.

In these places, the medicine men and chiefs held ceremonies. They would paint or draw pictures of animals to bring success in hunting. They ground ore and mixed it with animal fat to make paint mixtures of yellow or dark orange. They even used burned bones to make black paint.

Today, people can visit and explore famous caves and caverns in special parks all over the world. In some parks, lights brighten the way through the darkest, deepest parts of the cave systems. Guided tours can help people learn about the caves and the animals living in them.

Many caves and caverns are yet to be discovered. Their mysteries continue to be hidden in the deep, dark twisting passages below the surface of the earth.

SPELUNKING

Supplies a Good Caver Needs

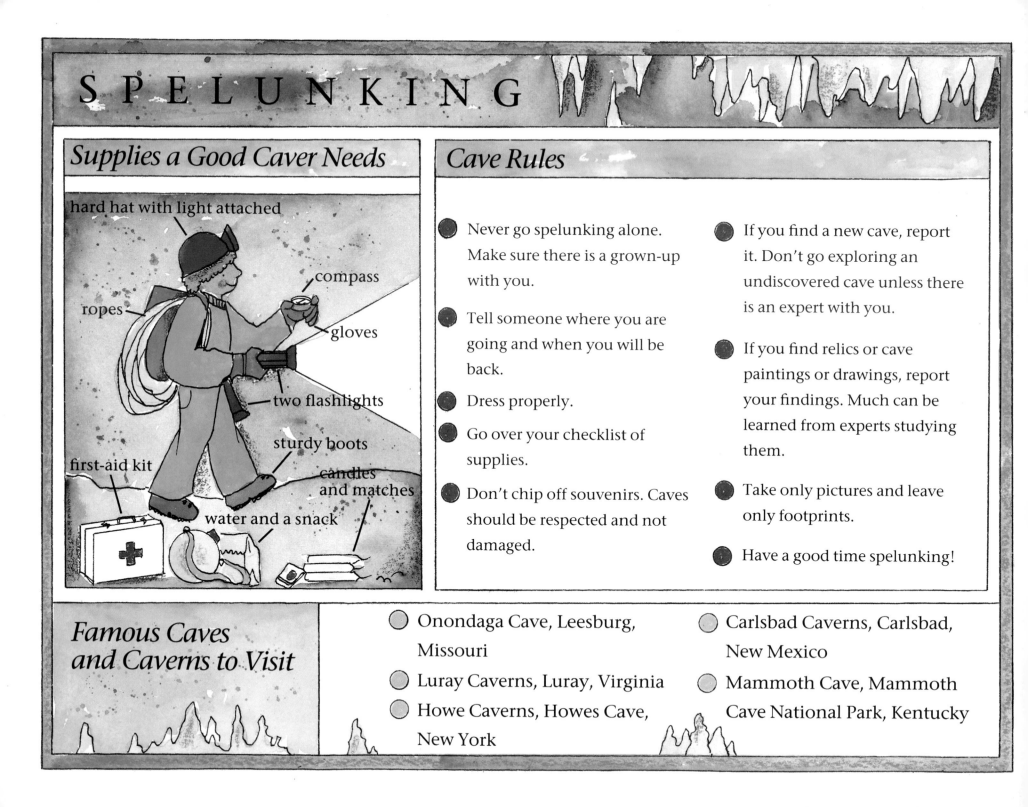

- hard hat with light attached
- ropes
- compass
- gloves
- two flashlights
- first-aid kit
- sturdy boots
- candles and matches
- water and a snack

Cave Rules

- Never go spelunking alone. Make sure there is a grown-up with you.
- Tell someone where you are going and when you will be back.
- Dress properly.
- Go over your checklist of supplies.
- Don't chip off souvenirs. Caves should be respected and not damaged.
- If you find a new cave, report it. Don't go exploring an undiscovered cave unless there is an expert with you.
- If you find relics or cave paintings or drawings, report your findings. Much can be learned from experts studying them.
- Take only pictures and leave only footprints.
- Have a good time spelunking!

Famous Caves and Caverns to Visit

- Onondaga Cave, Leesburg, Missouri
- Luray Caverns, Luray, Virginia
- Howe Caverns, Howes Cave, New York
- Carlsbad Caverns, Carlsbad, New Mexico
- Mammoth Cave, Mammoth Cave National Park, Kentucky